THE
PRESENT
PARENT
HANDBOOK

FAMILIUS

Published by Familius LLC, www.familius.com

Familius books are available at special discounts for bulk pur-
chases, whether for sales promotions or for family or corporate
use. For more information, contact Familius Sales at 559-876-
2170 or email orders@familius.com.

Library of Congress Cataloging-in-Publication Data
2016962613

Print ISBN 9781945547133
Ebook ISBN 9781945547522
Hardcover ISBN 9781945547539

Printed in the United States of America

Edited by Julia Levitan
Cover design by David Miles
Book design by Brooke Jorden

10 9 8 7 6 5 4 3 2 1

First Edition

THE
PRESENT
PARENT
HANDBOOK

26
SIMPLE TOOLS TO DISCOVER THAT
THIS MOMENT, THIS ACTION,
THIS THOUGHT, THIS FEELING IS
EXACTLY WHY I AM HERE.

TIMOTHY DUKES, PHD

For my son,
Hunter Brooks Dukes

Contents

The Present Parent

Up until this very moment,
you have done the best job you could as a parent.
Start over today. Don't look back.
Show up for this moment.

Ask your child's eyes.
Be willing to feel everything,
and your heart will teach you all
that you need to know about parenting.

INTRODUCTION

Having a child in your life is one of the greatest challenges you will face. It is also an extraordinary opportunity to embrace the blessings that their presence brings. Bringing a life into the world and raising a child in that world is one of our most creative acts. Few actions have such far-reaching ramifications. Whatever feelings arise, welcome them all. Find within yourself the understanding that your children are precious gifts. Find the courage to accept them just as they are.

The essential qualities of the "Present Parent" can only be acquired through the process of being present. These abilities are developed, maintained, and improved as we evolve during the everyday demands of parenthood.

Where to start? Greet the great mystery of parenting with an open heart. By following some general guidelines, a foundation for presence can be established. This book has been written as a reference guide to be kept by your bedside to refresh and inspire you as you spend your moments, hours, days, and years parenting your children.

Though I provide many tools that will help you become a more present parent, the best tool is your heart. When it's not working well, you will find yourself disconnected from your children, as in the following scenario.

Walking along a bike path on a beautiful spring morning, I pass a park where an army of children play. Their parents orbit around them, coffee cups in their hands, cell phones to their ears, text messages flying into the unknown like startled pigeons. As I watch, another parent meanders by on his bike with a mesh-enclosed cart in tow, his younger child inside bobbing side to side in a state of pre-sleep discontent. The older child, perhaps six years old, rides beside his dad on a tiny two-wheeler. The boy seems accustomed to this experience, alone and waiting for the attention of his father. The dad—Bluetooth in ear—remains fully engaged in a discussion with someone who, unbeknownst to him or her, is stealing his presence from his children.

Unfortunately, we've all been there and done that. What is the cost of these lost parenting opportunities?

After raising my son into adulthood with my wife and working with hundreds of clients as a psychotherapist over the years, I offer a simple perspective: if you can recognize that your child needs to be witnessed, held, and loved by you, he or she will have a chance to thrive.

Aside from what our current consumer culture wants us to believe, our children don't need more stuff. They need us, and they need our presence. Parent love is rather simple; it is a place in the heart that breathes life into the child's experience and helps them to find their place in the world.

I hope to inspire you to rethink and retool how you feel about parenting. I encourage you to give yourself permission to be exactly who you are. At the same time, I hope that you will both claim and grow into your unique way of embracing your children. This book has been developed out of years of witnessing the parent-child relationship in my clinical practice and simply observing parents with their children, including my own revelations with my wife and son. I realized that many of the challenges we face in modern society—environmental neglect, corporate greed, and the education gap—stem from a lack of parenting and a family wound.

I began to understand how numerous situational, societal, and environmental influences work to interrupt a parent's ability to relate to his or her child. I recognized that as parents, we have a deep desire to be the best parents we can while at the same time we fear that what we are doing is not good enough. I particularly wondered how these emotions could affect a parent's ability to relate to and pay attention to their child. Finally, I asked how—in spite of these circumstantial and emotional hindrances—parents become present for their children and the experience of parenting.

When I first considered the possibility of parenthood, I was confronted with a sense of aloneness and terror. I realized that I really did not know what it would mean to be a parent. I had no idea what to expect. Doubt, fear, confusion, and a host of conflicting feelings arose right along with pride and joy.

When I actually became a parent, I plunged headlong into the unknown. As beautiful and enriching as the experience was, a deep and unexpected pain also arose. Feelings of love were shadowed by the terror of loss. With the new life came a new fear of death. Parenting kindled the smoldering embers of a childhood lived long ago. Memories of myself as a child with my own parents burned through many of my interactions with my son. For better or worse, my parents live inside me, figures that remain deep within my heart.

In a very real way, we have to be willing to live with our questions and not get stuck in seeking answers; parenting is not a problem to be fixed. There is not a formula that when mastered will be effective in every situation.

The key to parenting lies in our willingness to learn, through our experiences of parenting, what it means to be a parent. The practical how-to is this: *listen deeply to yourself as you are revealed in your child's experience of you.* He or she speaks a language that is constantly refreshing itself. It is seldom known or easily understood, but it is always informative.

To parent a child is both simple and difficult. You must listen and be willing to feel. Trust that at any given moment, your child's voice will bring you closer to the parent you hope to be; this is your next opportunity to know your child and to understand yourself. This is the moment to be present.

What Is Presence?

Present: the here and now.

Presence: the state or fact of existing, occurring, or being present in a place or thing.

Staying present requires practice. It requires the capacity to balance your thoughts, feelings, and behaviors with your child's internal world. Presence allows you to be aware of your thoughts as they arise before your emotions pull your attention away and dislocate you from your child.

Presence is a fundamental act of empathic attunement that allows us to fully engage instead of simply appearing to pay attention while inwardly redirecting our awareness. This allows us to value intimate moments of play instead of wishing we were back at the office or gym. Presence allows us to embrace our child even when our attention is compelled elsewhere. This is the practice of presence.

When I am present, I can see, smell, hear, and feel my child. As I think of my son intermittently throughout the day, even when he is far away, presence determines how dynamically I am able to experience him.

How do our children find this residency within us? We look at our children when they are sleeping and are aware of our feelings. We see the smiles on their faces when they first greet us in the morning, and if we are present, we are aware of this as a unique moment. When we smell our child's head as we hug, we are aware of the scent. When we feel the texture of their skin, we rest within the warmth of the embrace. When we taste the salt on our child's face as we kiss their sweaty cheeks, we are grateful to be so close. We have both the experience and the awareness of the experience; we are the witness as well as the partici-pant. We feel whole as the moment reverberates with great power. Presence provides not a way beyond but a way through life as it unfolds moment to moment. These seeds of enlightenment rest within each moment of parenting.

Some say that the parent-child bond is a result of "quality time," which is not determined by the amount of time a parent and child spend together but rather by what they do during this time. While this quality time does have an important effect, and is a form of presence, I believe that deeper bonds are formed and maintained due to the amount of incidental time we spend with our children.

The baby needs her parent to pick up her discarded spoon time after time as she experiments with tasting her food and learning to manipulate the world around her. The two-year-old wants his dad to simply sit with him on the floor, helping him stack blocks into a fort that he will soon destroy—just because he can. The adolescent needs her mom to smile with pride as she turns to see if Mom noticed her brilliant maneuver on the basketball court. In these seemingly incidental moments, the fibers of the par-ent's attention weave gently into the child's psyche.

As we begin to develop into present parents, we become consistently located in our child's world. Parenting is a creative act, deeply affecting the development of our children as we involve and evolve ourselves in the shaping and preservation of their lives.

Parenting is an opportunity to start fresh each day. If we choose to take on the responsibility, we are free to be mindful and present. Sometimes we invent ourselves on a moment-to-moment basis. As we do this, parenthood is uncovered, recovered, and discovered in our own experience as well as in our child's.

Present parenting is a path with heart. The heart has a soft voice that whispers its sorrows in hidden shadows and bursts with joy in radiant displays. It is also fleeting, choosing to shy away from what might be too strongly interpreted or judged. Our hearts are layered deeply within for safekeeping. Suffering and sorrow are understood to be as relevant to parenting as joy and happiness, and this discomfort is really okay. Our task is to find meaningful ways to make use of this discomfort so that it only enhances and deepens the connection.

When things are difficult, when futility reigns and you lose touch with the intimate feelings you hold for your child, this depth of commitment will sustain you. It is the rare and precious realization that what has come into your life cannot be undone. Once you become a parent, you are forever a parent.

Each moment with your child is a fresh opportunity to relate and participate. As parents, we must constantly mediate the forces that could distance us from our children, such as work, conflict, and trauma. The tasks involved do not form an easy path to follow, but we must try.

As parents, we become the embodiment of the choices we make in each moment. These choices shape us. When a present parent greets his child, bathes him, holds him, prepares his meals, picks up his toys, sits with him at a table for a meal, or plays with him in the yard, he enters the *child's world*. Physical presence is key, yet it is only one aspect of the complex psychological, emotional, behavioral, and relational posturing that is involved in being *with* our children. A present parent sustains her ability to relate. She is cognizant of the power that she has in her child's life and is able to foster their separate realities while holding on to their joint interactions.

Parent presence holds and nourishes life as well as mediates and manages struggle for the child. As parents, when we hold presence for our children, we are both the container and the contained. We hold that moment so that the beauty of who we are as parents becomes part of the formation of our children in a safe and facilitated context. When we play, we ensure their freedom and safety.

When they ask us a question, we respond and keep the question alive while joining their wonderment and curiosity. When we have a family meal, we set the context for them to receive nourishment and nurturing while we become a part of what they consume. This is how we hold the container of home.

Being present for our children requires our willingness to adapt and adjust in subtle, dynamic ways. It is in our presence that our children learn to know who they are in the world. In any given moment, we have every opportunity to maintain a sanctuary to which our children can retreat, see who they are, and be themselves. We want our children to pursue this process of self-discovery with us, not in a world that awaits them just outside the safety of our presence.

A.1

Pay Attention

Children grow well in the soil of our attention. They look for us to provide nourishment as they blossom. They sink roots in our love and see their own reflection in our eyes. They bask in the light of our attention. Our presence provides these vital conditions that hold our child in the center of our world and create a sense of continuity and safety.

Present parenting invites us to pause and unplug from external distractions—including jobs, errands, and other responsibilities. We don't *attend* to our children so that we can get back to our daily tasks; we attend to these tasks so that we can be with our children. The degree to which we are able to be with ourselves and attend to ourselves reflects the degree to which we are comfortable being with our children. Our children will always be our greatest mirrors.

A.2

LEARN TO **ADAPT**

Parenting is a process of adapting to a never-ending flow of change. As parents, we constantly undergo on-the-job training. Parental roles are no longer defined by or dependent upon traditional norms. Coming into parenthood can be a situation you find yourself in or something you planned. Every one of us is here because of our own unique situation. This calling—if you will—is unique to you and the choices you made to get here.

Each parent is expected to provide, nourish, and manage the household as well as their own lives. These challenging situations, in which a parent is caught between competing demands for time and attention, require mindfulness and the ability to manage transitions skillfully.

Choosing to be present demands that we also change our focus, attention, and awareness, all of which must adapt to the present needs of our children. Ask yourself who is best suited to adapt and compromise in any given moment: you, your partner, or your child? Whose expectations will be met and whose will be put aside? Navigating these situations is vital to present parenting.

Children are very adaptive, and we need to be equally adaptive to be present for them. Your child can be a bird one moment, a baby girl the next, and then suddenly a superhero. She can have her feelings hurt and then play happily moments later. You may notice that when your child is suffering, his or her ability to adapt is temporarily constricted. Parents are no different. If you enter your child's day locked inside your mood and unwilling to be open to the unexpected, you will soon encounter a challenge. Having dynamic choice with your children and a willingness to feel and adapt bodes well for a healthy relationship.

What happens when you're not feeling so upbeat about a situation? Stay honest. Don't put on a "happy face" in an attempt to adapt. It won't be convincing to any child. Don't suppress how you are feeling. Instead, adapt the way you incorporate your emotional state, which will demand some vulnerability. Recognize that each time you enter your child's world, you are crossing a threshold. Consider yourself a guest in your child's world, and each moment, enter with the intention to add value. If you need extra time before you cross over into their world, negotiate a walk, a shower, a change of clothes, or a snack. Take a few moments to breathe and settle before you engage. Find a way to manage your state of mind so that it syncs with your family. In other words, find the best way to go with the flow because you cannot expect your child to adjust to *you* if you are not in control of yourself.

This might sound daunting, but we do not need to meet these situations in isolation. This is a challenge that the whole family can face together. Through communication and collaboration, we can find a way to transition so that no one is left feeling disappointed. Home and work life can coexist. There is no reason why one side of our life needs to eclipse the other.

TIPS FOR SUCCESSFUL ADAPTATION

- **Allow for the unexpected** and be willing to adjust.
- **Set clear time and behavioral boundaries** and be willing to renegotiate these boundaries.
- **Make your intentions predictable.** Let those around you know what you are doing and how long you intend to be doing it. Say "not now, but

in twenty or thirty minutes" or "once I have fin-
ished this email." Then deliver on your promise.

Every day is a new day. As our children evolve, present
parenting demands that we continuously explore changing frontiers. To do this, we must be willing to accept our
child's experience as is, not as we would like it to be. As
we parent, we are often managing unseen forces, trying
to balance challenges for which we are not prepared and
doing the best we can to keep our child at the center.

Our children not only live in our world; they also
develop simultaneously in two worlds: the inner and the
outer. What may look like a withdrawal from one may
actually be an engagement with the other. Only a small
part of a child's development is visible. They may reject
something today but embrace it tomorrow. We must learn
how to navigate the uncharted territory of our child's
unknowable world.

B

KEEP THE **BALANCE**

I magine that you are on one end of a teeter-totter and your child is on the other. Balance is achieved when the seesaw gently moves up and down as you both make small adjustments. Balance takes a delicate touch, patience, and a consistency that is maintained by your presence.

What about the emotional teeter-totter of real life? The one that demands our participation even when we have our hands full and are not feeling particularly balanced? Like the moment when he—for some reason—does not want you to change his diaper, or the unexpected, heartbreaking sadness that explodes when she is not invited to a friend's birthday party. The smallest and most unpredictable event can feel insurmountably disturbing. In these moments, your child's suffering naturally tips the balance in your relationship.

Achieving balance requires adjustment. Our children constantly face change that forces them to transform. To stay connected, we have to adjust our position on life's proverbial teeter-totter. We must find the ability and willingness to make these adjustments within ourselves. Whether they are large or small, these shifts help maintain a graceful balance for our children, ourselves, and the whole family.

We are their protector: an enclosing force that holds, balances, and guides. When the balance becomes uneven, it is up to us—not our children—to make the necessary adjustments to bring things back to scale. Our children do not need to "give in" or make things right. It is up to us, as parents, to navigate in a way that will empower rather than diminish them.

As with all things communicative, it's important to look at how you will address an imbalance. In many instances, it's so tempting to just say no and therefore reset the balance by stopping their current behavior. However, balance cannot be maintained with a negative attitude, response, judgment, or criticism. Those reactions actually tip the scale even more and take much longer to correct.

Many parents confuse balance for reciprocity. When I think of reciprocity, I think of a two-way street. If I am giving, then I might expect him to give back to me. If I listen, then she should be willing and able to listen as well.

It is not that everything is returned in kind but that there is an even flow. Although this might be true for some relationships, unfortunately, it is not true for parenting. If reciprocity is indeed a two-way street, then it's the parent's job to ensure that the flow is in the child's favor.

Reciprocity connotes fairness and a shared set of rules. However, we cannot expect our children to know how to be "fair" with us. Until they mature enough to understand their own feelings, they might not know—or even care—how we feel.

We usually think like this: *If I am free to expect something of you, then you should be free to expect something of me.* Again, this breaks down with children. My son needs me when he needs me, not when I decide that I am available. However, when I need him, for the most part, it should be when he is able and willing to be available.

Reciprocity suggests that you do something because you expect a certain result in kind. However, life with your child is not intended to be reciprocal. For example, when you have an argument, it does not unfold in equal measure. Parents can't play by the same rules, because what is fair for us is secondary to what is fair for our child. Using our emotions to manage our child's emotions starts a battle that no one will win. It is our job to manage the relationship so that it works; moving through a situation and staying together is what is important. The willingness to give without receiving—because you understand what is truly at stake—is true reciprocity.

When you assert yourself in terms of "this is right" and "that is wrong," you have negated the natural balance of your relationship with your child. When your child mispronounces a word, interrupts a conversation, acts "silly," or puts himself at risk and you directly confront him with a negative, he will either wilt or push back with greater force. In either case, the balance is tipped. This is not necessarily a problem, but it does require that someone take responsibility for correcting the imbalance and work to bring the relationship back into alignment.

In the parent-child relationship, opposition, disintegration, and the restoration of balance are integral aspects of parent-child development. It's natural—and necessary—for children to get under their parents' skin sometimes, but we must be willing to accommodate these intrusions and momentary possessions.

If your son is an infant and moving his body in your embrace, do you adjust your hold so that he is more comfortable or does he shift to fit better in your arms? From the earliest interaction between you and your child, your relationship is negotiated. If the two of you are walking down the street hand in hand, there are countless moments of tension—she tugs you, you pull her away from traffic, you walk faster, she walks slower. Who ultimately determines how you move together? How this tension is negotiated, balanced, and resolved is the basic ground of parenting.

As we take on the responsibility to manage this balance, we must make every adjustment we are capable of so that our children do not grow up one-sided—either so inflated and demanding that our ability to respond diminishes over time or so small that we hardly notice their weight in relation to our own drives. The one-sided child seeks his completion as he tries to discover himself in his adult world. The two-sided child evolves into a balanced adult because he has you, his parent, teaching him through example how to accommodate and develop under the changing demands of each moment.

CONSCIOUS INTENTION

With conscious intention, the present parent is capable of staying present while mediating his discordant thoughts, desires, and competing demands for attention. Presence requires that when we parent, we remember to hold a conscious intention regardless of how this feels in our head, our body, or our relationship. We actually have to remind ourselves to do this.

In every moment with our children, conscious intention allows a "co-flow" to weave throughout the day. When we are conscious and intend to remain connected to our children, we flow like two streams interlacing. Each overlap is determined by our intention to be present.

When my child was very young and just making sense of things around him, he asked me, "Why . . . you always angry?" To him, my concentrated expression made me look angry. He must have watched me countless times before making that determination. A fact of life, you may say, but it's illustrative of how a parent's state of mind can be disruptive to a child's state and how, without conscious intention, the child is left to sort out the meaning.

Before you walk through the door, join in a conversation, or sit down in the playroom, consider this: your mood, temperament, thoughts, and feelings will most often be on different tracks. Your presence will always change what was there before you arrived. It may or may not be for the better, depending on who is making the accommodations to bring your world into accord with your child's world. Always ask yourself, "Am I ready for the change that is about to come?"

AFFIRMATIONS OF CONSCIOUS INTENTION

- ⟿ With conscious intention, I am able to bring energy, interest, availability, and curiosity to each encounter with my child.
- ⟿ With conscious intention, it's easier to maintain focus, concentration, and mindfulness.
- ⟿ With conscious intention, my capacity for empathy, compassion, joy, and kindness expands.
- ⟿ With conscious intention, I am able to be more upbeat, present, and relaxed, giving my child a better chance to be himself or herself.

Constant
Communication

Children are natural communicators. They are always letting us know that they are present and in need of our attention. They will blossom if we are able and willing to recognize that this is exactly how life should be. Children communicate their presence without reservation, unless they are taught to think and behave otherwise. They need to be received and to know that they are being received. This is genuine communication.

If I want to communicate with my child, I must first make sure that he can hear me and that I have his attention. Then I need to listen, make sure I am connected, and be certain that there is some basis of interest in what I am saying.

When children are young, it may take extra focus to make sense of what very often sounds like gibberish. We have to respect their current language pattern while gently teaching them a rounder and fuller means of self-expression. It may take many, many iterations for us to fully understand them. Patience is the key. Communication will happen only when we make the monumental adjustments necessary to listen fully to our children. Agree to be with your child where she is developmentally instead of foisting your language demands upon her or becoming impatient when your expectations are not being adequately met. If we want to teach our children how to communicate, we need to listen and let them know that they are being heard.

Unfortunately, a lot of our "communication" is in service of alienation and control, not in service of connection. This can be confusing to a child. "I'm sorry for being late; there was so much traffic" communicates to your child that you have other priorities. "I'm sorry I am late and that I didn't prioritize my schedule correctly" is often more true than a multitude of excuses. Your child may actually understand this. More than likely, they already know that it's true.

Let them know where you stand so that what they already know can be confirmed: express how you feel, account for your moods, and tell them about your day and the challenges you have faced. Keep them updated on the logistics for the week so that the whole family can be best prepared.

Be accountable for how you feel and communicate this at every opportunity. Don't make your problem your child's problem. Allow your behavior to mirror your feelings, and your children will learn to do the same. It is too easy to assume that if you have a problem with your child, it has everything to do with them. Examine yourself in the situation. Expand your viewpoint to determine what is actually at play, and seek what is true in the moment.

Communication is a living process. We grow right alongside our children, and we mirror each other's experiences. When we see their smiling faces, we respond and communicate through our own facial expressions. Our loving smile tells them that they have a place within us.

As we communicate our love, they learn the complexity of that language and immediately open to a capacity to express the same. This mirror effect also applies when negative emotions are expressed. As we communicate our distance, preoccupation, anger, frustration, or judgment, our children have the capacity to feel these emotions as well. These dynamics of communication continue through every moment and every stage of their development. How we respond becomes increasingly complex as our children grow.

I recall a very brief interaction between a parent and his son. The boy snatched something out of his parent's hand. "Don't snatch!" the parent admonished, snatching it right back. If you want your child to control himself, you need to control *yourself*. You cannot expect your child to behave when you are exhibiting bad behavior.

Practice what you preach. This may take time, and at first, you may not make the right decisions. Model for your children that you are able to assess a situation and respond appropriately, maturely, and wisely. Ironically, there is no better time to do this than when you are in conflict with one another.

Simply reacting in a moment has very little influence when it comes to communication. Telling a child something once—"don't snatch"—does not register as learning. Communication must be held and cultivated as a living process. By engaging authentically with an open heart and mind, this fundamental communication pattern becomes the template for our children's future relationships. If we want our children to become good communicators, we need to meet them at every turn. Listening to them and responding with full presence is like the sculptor's interaction with clay: the form is created as a result of the sculptor's intention, and simultaneously, his intention is shaped by his interaction with the clay.

We have a choice in *how* we communicate, and our communication is often defined by its impact on those around us. There is no place to hide from our children. Where would we go so that they could not see us, feel us, and experience every nuance of who we are? We must be aware of what is really taking place in a moment, and as our children experience our attempt to communicate in an authentic way, they learn to do the same. The conditioned, unconscious behavior of the parent is brought to consciousness through the child's ability to mimic and experiment.

As we keep our attention tuned in to our children's world and listen deeply to their struggles, a reassuring voice can encourage them to lean forward into life. "Go ahead; you can do it." In the same breath, our voice can be a reminder that they have a place to return. "I am right here if you need me."

To prepare for the future, we must build a strong foundational presence now. It is not an option to sit back and watch as our child's life evolves out of our view. We must communicate that the world of the parent is progressing at a similar rate to the world of the child. Although we may not understand what kind of world they will ultimately face, we can make every effort to stay present, a steady and solid rock as their lives unfold.

Communicating presence allows our children to find both the way in and the way back. If she knows there is a place waiting, she is most likely to also trust you are there. She feels safe. She knows how to both stretch her wings and land on her feet. She has done so a thousand times only to discover you patiently waiting.

TIPS FOR SUCCESSFUL COMMUNICATION

- **Go easy on having too many rules.** It is not so much what is communicated but how.

- **Know that sometimes doing nothing is the best choice.** Trust that many things will simply pass by or resolve on their own.

- **On the other hand, time will not mend all situations.** Don't wait too long to set things straight when your communication creates an imbalance.

- **Find a way to keep things flowing between you, your partner, and your child or children.** As communication breaks down, the natural ease of being together becomes stilted.

↬ **Don't try to hide your true emotions.** Like a river, everything we think, feel, express, or withhold flows into the landscape of our family. There is no place to hide, so settle down and be willing to participate in making things work for you and your loved ones.

Stay **Devoted**

When you are a devoted parent, you will find that in each moment, there is an opportunity to embrace your experience, even if it's painful. It is painful when you see that your child is disappointed. It is painful when you realize one day that your infant will no longer make those soft murmuring sounds. It is painful when you leave your child on his first day of school. The difference between the pain of presence and that of absence is determined by one fundamental characteristic—when you are present, you are the one who manages the discomfort.

Devotional parenting requires surrendering and staying present regardless of the mess. When something causes you to feel dislocated—your car needs new tires and it's not within your budget—you need to process your frustration outside of your relationship with your children and not allow your connection with them to be broken. If things do break down, simply reconnect as soon as possible. Reach out, receive, and be held by someone who loves you without question. You don't need to know how; just devote yourself: show up and participate in what is waiting for you.

Once the smoke clears and you can see the situation with the benefit of distance, you will notice that this is not, in fact, a war between parent and child. It is a struggle that you are having with your own sense of responsibility, control, and accountability. Parental devotion requires engagement, surrender, balance, and a willingness to facilitate each moment into the next.

Only insofar as the parent opens to his or herself and is willing to process difficult emotions can the child find her way within their relationship. When we begin to experience ourselves as a *part* of our children, we offer our children the opportunity to realize they are a part of us. As we surrender, we allow our child to flourish, to fully create herself in our attention instead of molding herself into who she thinks we need her to be.

BE DISPENSABLE

There is something in the interplay between absence and presence that informs us of what it means to parent. Though a child needs his or her parent's presence, he or she may also need a parent's understandable absence. Different aspects of psychological, emotional, and physical development may occur in the context of paternal absence—like the critical ability to differentiate oneself. When my son has a feeling or a thought, he wants it to be his feeling, his thought. I am not permitted to touch it without his consent. For example, when he tells me about reading a classic book that was also important to me, I have to listen and let it be his. I have to join his world and not ask him to join my world. He wants and needs me to witness his discovery and marvel at how wonderful it is. It is not the time to share one of my experiences in an attempt to let him know that I understand; I can relate; I get it. For him, this would reduce his experience and cause him to pull away.

Parenting requires that we accept being left behind and forgotten only to be retrieved and remembered later. At every stage of development, we need to accept that we are dispensable in our child's world. This is most clearly illustrated in how we play with our children and how those interactions change over time. Play is the ultimate creative act, and it is in acting creatively that we discover ourselves and one another.

These whimsical interactions can take many forms: playful teasing or banter, a card trick, or a fake in basketball. In these moments, our children are reminded of our presence and affection. The push-and-pull nature of play allows you to come and go in your child's world, allowing them to become more deeply rooted in their independence and personality. In play, they can afford to let you go and still be assured of your return.

As we release our children, we participate in strengthening their ability to find their way in the world, and as they release us, they allow us to find our way as well. In any given moment, we can discover the right measure of our embrace and presence. Some mild restraint by the parent may be met with laughter and squeals. Too much tension, and the child may feel overwhelmed. This is a challenge for every parent at every stage of development. We need to devote ourselves fully in one moment and then in the next completely let go.

EXPERIENCE THE WOUNDS

As a present parent, we are given an opportunity to heal the scars from our own childhood. By staying present, even as we experience our wounds from the past, we can actually heal.

Where does this pain come from? Often it arises unexpectedly, when you are unconsciously missing your own parent and feeling the pain of their absence. That little child still lives inside you, crying out for love. Confusion arises when feelings of sadness, irritation, anger, or impatience activate "out of nowhere." If you are willing to feel the anguish of the past while remaining present for your child in the moment, healing is more likely.

If you grew up without a parent present, then you grew up with his or her absence. Questioning whether you even know how to parent, you may approach your parenthood with trepidation. Even after all the years of therapy, soul-searching, meditation, and education, an absent parent—my father—still lives within me. What he gave me, because of his unwillingness or inability to feel, was his absence. The seed of my father's discontent lives within me, and when watered with my resentment, it breaks my heart one more time. As a result, I wonder how much of him I have become.

In the moments when I choose to be present, something constellates that incrementally replaces my father's absence. As I father, I am fathered. The archetype of parenting emerges in the ground of my heart, and the void left by my father's absence has healed within me. His absence has contributed to how I make sense of my world and how I have come to help my son make sense of his.

As we become parents, the memories of our own parents meld into our experience, and this intergenerational presence deeply informs us. Many adults look back on their childhood and discover the scars left from absent parenting. This may not always be a conscious memory; more likely, it is maintained as a vague notion that something was just not right. Perhaps our journey as parents is to somehow locate and recover what we never actually had. Being a present parent for our children can help us to do this.

The present parent has the capacity to tolerate discordant experiences. Each act of parenting is an opportunity to release the pain of unfolding memories as well as an opportunity for the child to find acceptance and grow in the experience of his parent. Absence is immediately equated with a loss of love. If we are not there for our children, it is a small step for them to conclude that we do not love them. Thankfully, many of us learn how to parent by doing just what our parents did not do.

A parent's absence resides in a deep part of ourselves and—like an unwelcome guest—stops in for a visit. We do not forget or outlive these painful memories. They remain in residence in the unconscious and will surface from time to time with the potential to inform or torment us. We can't give our wounds back, but we can accept them as part of our growth and as a reminder to parent differently, with more consciousness, kindness, patience, and love.

We must learn to embrace these memories, little by little, and allow our grief to inform both our current and future interactions with our children. If we begin at their birth, we can develop patterns of caring and closeness and learn to manage those patterns that restrict us. Painful memories arise right along with the positive experiences of parenting; to deny one simply diminishes the other.

We all want to do right by our children in ways that our parents could not. It seems absurd to think that our parents didn't want the very best for us—they did. Their challenges laid the very foundation for us to face similar obstacles with a greater sense of understanding and opportunity.

Growing up with an absent parent creates infinite forks in the road: one direction pulling like gravity toward any kind of parental connection, the other rebelling against all things parental. When our parent is not present, we seek him or her in all things. We might seek them in other relationships or in our obsessions, substance abuse, self-abuse, or other problematic behavior. When our parent is off in a place that we cannot see nor comprehend, we will suffer and falsely seek resolution outside ourselves. We are compelled to seek ourselves in others, because as children, we were denied the opportunity to be ourselves. Filling that void is a potent experience, but the quest to "find" an absent parent can inhibit a child's ability to truly know himself or herself.

Parenting, though painful, requires that we learn to include ourselves when we are needed and remove ourselves when our presence is unwanted. There is a moment-by-moment balance between staying the course and letting go. You can learn to notice your own absence as you recognize the pain of the absent parent in your heart. You can even transform this pain into love: love your child to heal yourself.

Love your children in your own way. Just be sure that your love frees them to have their love and their life so that they are supported and not impeded.

Sometimes it's not easy to know when I've been absent. I don't want to lie to myself and pretend that I have been the best parent possible. The truth is that I often don't know. This is the inheritance from my absent father: a heart that lives in question. It is within my heart that my son exists. If I choose to let my child see himself within my heart, I have to believe that he will experience my presence.

Life with our children, for all of its richness, is ultimately very complex. When we interact with our child, we are not only dealing with their behavior and what is in front of us; we are reminded of how we were treated by our parents, siblings, and just about everyone who participated in our development. We are confronted with the influence of friends, cultural dictates, and expectations as well as the influences of our partner and the complexity of their family history. Everything having to do with being a parent is steeped in a stew of past, present, and future parental influences.

FIND FULFILLMENT

The opportunity for fulfillment lives in every moment that we are present with our children. When we can put the laptops down, turn off the phone, and connect in a sincere and authentic way, there is no greater sense of presence. We can even lower our heart rates and stress levels when we come into this place, surrendering everything else on the to-do list—which can wait.

In such a precious and rare moment, we get to experience perhaps the deepest form of love. With our children, we can seek this kind of fulfillment in the subtlest ways: looking deeply into their eyes, feeling the warmth of their skin, listening to the joy in their voice. Let your child know then and there how much you love them and how much this moment means to you. It is in this recognition that children understand that they exist, as they are witnessed, received, and affirmed by the parent. Something sacred is completed, connected, and ultimately fulfilled.

Tips to Increase Your Capacity for Fulfillment

- ↬ **Learn her smiles.** How many does she have?
- ↬ **Watch his hands** and how they move to the rhythm of his speech.
- ↬ **Notice the sound of her voice** when she is excited.
- ↬ **Hold and be still** as his melancholy dampens the mood between you.
- ↬ **Hold your tongue** when what she says seems all but impossible.
- ↬ **Watch his eyes** and notice when they light up.
- ↬ **Remember every moment** is their moment as much as yours.
- ↬ **As you depart, stop and turn back to look** at what you are about to leave.
- ↬ **Hold on to the entire moment.** You have the capacity to experience your child, partner, and family all at once.
- ↬ **Take pride in your parenthood as it is.** When it is not enough, know that you can improve it by practicing presence.

↬ **Fill up with joy.** This is one time to overindulge! When you are joyful, your children will also benefit.

The nuances necessary to be present in the moment require a consciousness with a capacity for compassion, love, and deep empathy. Yes, you can be present, and you are capable of great love.

GIFTING CONSCIOUSNESS

ifting consciousness is a term I use for the process of unspoken, reciprocal, and respectful communication. Being conscious of the family, an individual member, the dog, or the surrounding plants replenishes the larger landscape cultivated through gifting consciousness.

If we are willing to be present parents, our children will find a way to receive what they need from us, and hopefully, we will receive what we need from them. The presence and consciousness we bring to our relationships with our children defines our ability to parent.

Our children know on a deeper level that when we truly acknowledge their presence, they are part of the content forming our conscious reality. Through holding presence, we are able to offer the gift of our awareness. In turn, we receive the recognition that the life we hold, recognize, and feel is also able to hold, recognize, and feel us.

I am aware of you, child. You, child, are aware of me.

I see you, child. And you see me.

All of life is available for our awareness when we attend with consciousness to its form. In any given moment, I can offer my child the gifts of my attention: care, love, understanding, curiosity, joy, interest, time, humor, patience, respect, embrace, vulnerability, proximity, trust, allegiance, agreement, and so many more. Life with my child is not simply something for me to react to; for me, it presents an opportunity to give in each new moment.

I try to imagine what it must be like for parents who feel alienated from their children. I know many who do, and I hear their sad stories. In those moments, I am grateful for this one simple understanding: children will always gift us with their presence. They are a part of who we are. We need to feel our feelings without the expectation that things could, would, or should be different. This is the gift of being present.

HOLD THE PIECES TOGETHER

hildren tell lies for very different reasons, and it's important to consider the impetus before reacting to the lie itself. Consider if your child is "lying" to manipulate the situation to get his or her own way or if your child is trying to protect something that isn't ready to be revealed. If it's the latter, your child is using the best strategy he or she has in the moment to hold their world together. What emerges as half-truth or incomplete reasoning may simply be the best iteration manageable at the time. Confronting a lie in your child is tricky business. It's important to hold the different pieces of the puzzle together before determining how to respond.

Something is broken in the kitchen, and you just know your child is responsible, but when you ask, she says, "I have no idea what happened." He returns from school without his lunchbox, and when you ask, he tells you,

"Someone stole it." There is a new scratch in your car door, and she tells you it was there before she drove it. You ask if he brushed his teeth, and he says, "Yes!"—but you can still see the blueberry stains of the lollipop. In all of these cases, you are confronted with two pieces of information: your own observations and assumptions versus what your child says is true.

The smallest thing can fracture a child's equilibrium. Children hide what they want or need to keep private, and when they are in this space, the equilibrium of trust is disrupted. They lock us out of their world temporarily. We feel this wall, and it doesn't feel good. We want in, but we need to respect their privacy until they feel safe enough for us to bear witness. A child caught in a web of his or her lies will eventually disclose the truth to a respectful, compassionate parent. By staying present and grounded and not forcing our children to reveal what is not yet ready to be shared, we gain their trust and help restore their equilibrium.

WHEN FACED WITH A LIE, ASK YOURSELF THESE SIMPLE QUESTIONS:

↪ **Does it really matter if what is hidden is revealed?** Confronting a lie just to "teach your child a lesson" is not always wise and rarely works. Ask yourself if you can manage the ambivalence of what your child is hiding from you.

- ⚬ **Is confronting the lie worth the cost to your child?** Sometimes when you confront a lie, you free your child of a tremendous burden; however, at other times, you create a defeat that can cause shame and self-loathing. Choose your battles wisely when confronting your child's defenses. Sometimes the cost—to yourself, your child, and your whole family—is too great.

- ⚬ **Can I give the lie time to reveal itself?** What if I do nothing and simply allow my child to lie? There is deep personal learning that accompanies the option to collude with an untrue statement. Sometimes it just comes down to timing; if you let it go, you can come around to confronting it when your child does not have so many defenses at play.

We are all adept at shaping our own versions of reality. When it involves your child, timing is everything. A child's world is fractured when there is a lie in it; yet, paradoxically, the lie serves to hold the pieces together. Your job is to help your child make their world whole and right again.

I

BE **INTERESTED** IN TRUTH

When you cut though all the feelings, psychology, and behaviors of parenting, there is something quite simple waiting for you—the truth.

One thing our children will inevitably catch us doing, from time to time, is not listening. "Dad, are you listening? Dad!" your young child might ask when only moments ago she was chattering merrily. Now she eyes you warily, her face stiff and her arms crossed. She caught you drifting away in your river of thoughts. What is true in this moment? She's angry and maybe disappointed. You could pretend you had been listening and repeat the echo of her words, or you could confess the truth.

This is a wonderful opportunity to demonstrate your authenticity. You're human, and your child needs to see that you are not always paying attention, so it's good that she caught you. If you are willing to go for what is true, simply acknowledge your absence and apologize: "Sorry, honey. Please tell me again; I was somewhere else." Then get on with the task at hand: parenting. The point is to validate her experience and what is true in those moments.

Cultivating trust between a child and parent is something that needs attention on a daily basis. Though trust may be embedded in the very nature of your relationship, if not cared for, it can be lost. If we are too busy, preoccupied, or neglectful of our children, we can quickly lose their trust.

Trust is simply the recognition that when we give to and receive the people we love, we are bound by these moments of mutual care. I hold part of you, and you hold part of me. It is very important to recognize that what I have received of yours, when returned to you, should be enhanced and not diminished. This is the basis of empathic attunement, mindful awareness, and a parent's presence.

At times, you may be paying attention to what your child needs but are unable to understand what your child is telling you. What is true in this situation? Take a risk. Communicate that you don't understand. Encourage your child to find another way to explain what he or she is saying. This will not only help you both navigate the conflict, it will also help him refine his communication skills and deepen the bond of trust between you. When you earnestly seek to understand your child, he or she can see it, hear it, and feel it. This is parent presence.

Going for what is true changes in every interaction with your child, and that constant shift requires that you manage your response without just reacting out of frustration.

"What would you like for dinner?" you ask.

"Nothing!" your child says and stomps out of the kitchen.

In this exchange, it's hard to determine what's really going on. Clearly, the moment to communicate without friction has been lost, but only temporarily. A parent may have many thoughts: *Is he too hungry to know? Is he disturbed by something I did or didn't do? Did something happen after school or in school?* You may never know. Yet what is *true* is that you have to meet your child's needs, which in this case means feeding him while co-managing his feelings and your own. This has to happen so that the next moment can unfold and the flow of life can be restored. All of this informs what is true in this moment and the actions needed to support it.

Truth is like a golden thread that runs through each moment. We follow it as best as we can, gently finessing the particulars of each new moment, so that what is true continues to reveal itself.

J.1

FIND **JUSTICE** IN CONSISTENCY

I n the spirit of practicality, we tell ourselves that if we establish rules and adequately enforce them, every-thing should work just fine. Rules help evoke justice, right? So we've been told again and again; however, justice has little to do with the rules we make and enforce as parents.

There's another way to institute justice—by establishing the only rule that matters: consistency. Of course, the rules of life do matter in order to keep our children safe: look both ways before you cross the street; don't leave with a stranger; wash your hands before you eat; etc. I'm referring to "the rules" we create out of a need to stay in control, rules which almost never work.

We've all heard someone say to a child, "Use your indoor voice!" What's wrong with this? Nothing from the outset. But by creating an arbitrary condition, you place the expectation on your children to adhere to a self-imposed rule when and if it is convenient for *you*. This is a difficult way to proceed in any relationship. Trying to maintain control strips the life right out of the situation.

What's the alternative? Your presence. Stay present during moments that make you want to reach for the rule book. I suggest consistently addressing each situation in real time, honoring and respecting your child's needs as they vary in any given situation. The rules in this case might fly out the door, and you might just be grateful. Presence becomes the only rule, and your presence becomes the fulcrum upon which consistency rests and where your child finds safety.

To a child, everything is an exploration and adventure. If you adopt this same attitude, you are giving your children the freedom to explore and develop. By focusing on consistency in behavior instead of strictly adhering to arbitrary rules, you allow your child to respond to each new situation independently. By letting go of control, you *empower* your child.

Consistency emerges when your interactions are predictable, uniform, and rich with relational life. Consistency is less about the message and more about the medium—not what you say but how you say it. If you maintain a consistent tone in your voice as you address your children, they will hear you. If you maintain a consistent place in your heart, they will know that they are not alone.

As with all communication practices, consistency is about building a loving and lasting connection with your child. Consistency holds your child's world together and makes it a safe and predictable environment.

By making our children's world predictable, they have a sense that each moment is supported by the one that came before. Can we help them understand that, as they face complex demands for their developing attention, they are not alone? If so, we are consistently doing everything that we can to maintain our connection. It is in this consistent connection that true justice prevails.

KEEP CONNECTED

Does distance really determine how deeply we care about our children? We've talked about some of the inner constraints and outer pressures that come with being a present parent. Yes, you have to chart a course between being together and being apart, carrying the responsibilities of being both the provider and nurturer. Sound daunting? At times, it is, but you are the Keeper of Connection and you *can* be present, even when you are far away or "don't have any time."

The present parent can learn to use the obstacles of time and space to their advantage. Any parent who is working, traveling, or otherwise engaged and away from their child will find themselves physically absent; however, this does not have to dislocate you. Although increments of time and space can be measured, distance does not determine how deeply we feel.

You can maintain presence by keeping connected, even when your child is not consciously aware that you are doing so.

TIPS FOR KEEPING CONNECTED

- ↪ **Know that whether or not you are physically present, you are connected to your child.** Reach deeply into your heart and hold your child in a place of love. You can be *anywhere* and send a message from your heart.

- ↪ **When you leave, make sure that your departure is predictable.** Give your child a frame of reference; for example, what time you are leaving, when you will be back, and where you will be. Use Google Maps to show exactly where you can be found.

- ↪ **While you are gone, send a few photos or a postcard from wherever you are.** A handwritten card or note is immediate and personal. Your children can get a glimpse of you in the world.

- ↪ **Spend time talking on the phone, video chatting, or texting.** Use video chat to read your child a story or help clean his or her room by talking through the process. Be available when your child needs you, not simply when it is convenient.

- ↬ **Stay involved with their schoolwork.** Keep a journal and include their teachers' names, the subjects they are taking, and the progress they are making.

- ↬ **Bring home a silly gift.** Even something small will remind your child that you were thinking of them.

- ↬ **Remember to spend time with your child when you first return home.** Make this first connection a priority, and call ahead so they can anticipate your arrival. Don't let calls, emails, or projects interfere with the moments of reconnection.

There may be times when you feel pulled out of orbit; when work or other obligations compromise your connection. Technology cannot be your only bridge. How do you maintain the connection with your children, maintain your presence, and hold on to the relationship even when you are physically distant? When you feel as though you are not doing enough, take the time to find out what you are missing and do something about it; this is as much for you as it is for your children.

Perfect parenting is a myth. No one is perfect, but you can be present. If what you are doing is missing the mark, try something else. Be compassionate, playful, and creative; trust that if you keep trying, you will find your way. There is no magic formula to parenting with presence, only the intention to do so.

Feel good about your plan to stay present, even when you are away. Take pride in how you manage yourself in relation to your child. Find a way to celebrate this intention every time you are called away. Remember how important it is for your child to have you in their world; you *and* your presence are a gift.

L.1

LISTEN AND
LEARN TO LET GO

Much of who I am today as a parent is rooted in my simple intention to listen, and I believe that so much of who my son has become emerges in his repeated discovery of himself in my presence. This discovery takes place in his thoughts, as he understands that I understand him. This discovery unfolds in his physical body, as he experiences the feelings of being bathed as an infant, wrestled with as a toddler, and embraced after winning his cross-country meet. This discovery brings clarity to his felt sense of belonging as he sees me recognize his contribution to our family in small and sometimes very large ways. By paying careful attention and putting myself aside, I learn how to lose my small needs in the moments that we are together and embrace the impact of his presence. I learn to let go, listen, and love in my own way in order to be present with him.

There are other opportunities to let go. Many of these are simply there to test your resolve or your boundaries. The only time to let go is when your child absolutely wants or needs you to. Letting go when you want to avoid feeling something difficult is not one of those times. Staying with your child in every moment and making the necessary adjustments to maintain the right amount of space is fine. Letting go because you have reached some imagined limit is not. If your child pushes you across the line, move the line and give yourself more space to stay with it.

Our internal world of thoughts, feelings, and memories can predetermine our ability to listen to what is actually being communicated. When we listen fully, there is very little separation between what we perceive as our internal world and that which is outside of us. At its roots, communication means to "make common." If our child communicates happiness and we fully listen, we have made common our willingness to receive that happiness. If our child communicates anger, we have indicated through our listening our willingness to share that anger. Through letting go and listening, we are able to fully participate in the narrative of our child's life.

How many interruptions have you already had simply trying to read this book? There is a comedic irony in focusing on a book about being a present parent and being simultaneously pulled away from the pages because of a million external factors.

As parents, it is up to us to listen, remain aware, and fine-tune our focus, concentration, and energy in relation to our children. We can't always rely on our partners to help. We won't always be around to know what pieces are at play. In any given moment, it is our responsibility to be mindful and sensitive to our children's ever-developing narrative with increasingly complex plotlines. It makes sense, then, to participate in the stories that they live.

Developing the art of listening is one way to be present. The other is to find a way to let go of or surrender your current position—your sense of fleeting time, your loss of focus, or any other common distractions that can move you away from being a present parent.

You can actually develop a practice of letting go while playing a board game with your child. Over the years of playing chess and other games with my son, I learned to maintain an even tension so that his victories were an extension of his current capacity: playing the edge of his knowledge, concentration, and skill. Through the years, the game of chess evolved in this tension, me adapting to his current level of play, letting go of my drive to win, holding the tension so that together and in common, we evolved and deepened our connection and play. I noticed, as a clinician and a parent, that if a child takes too many defeats, he will test his abilities elsewhere. I wanted my son to grow, develop, and struggle with me across the table and by his side. I didn't want him left to his own experimentations, and I didn't want him learning through defeat without my presence and support. Life presents plenty of opportunities for this in adulthood.

To defeat a child means that he loses his bargaining posture. In defeat, the relationship becomes one-sided and occurs at the child's expense by overpowering him, breaking him. However, if you simply let him win, there is the risk that you inadvertently abandon him. The task at hand is to hold and facilitate the tension so that it can run its course. The parent must be mindful to allow his or her child to determine that course.

Current societal messages often encourage us to place unachievable expectations on our children. The focus is all too often on winning. Gauge the pressure you place on your children. They will disconnect from you if you pressure them too much. Your best intention could, in fact, defeat them. They may submit, but do they truly benefit? If they push back, are you willing to take a defeat in service of your connection?

If you really want your children to be successful, make sure they have the necessary support and resources to meet the challenge. If the situation is not working for them, let this be an opportunity for you to correct it so that what they face is not defeat but an opportunity to learn by success. Be willing and ready to provide your children with what is missing: a heartfelt explanation or the patience to figure out their next move.

Correction is a subtle adjustment to any course of action. It allows children to once again flow freely and in accord with their surroundings, and it unlocks blocks and liberates them of their frustrations. They need you to bump up against, to test out who they are today, right now in this moment. They need to struggle with you, and sometimes you will defeat them. It is okay to do this, but make sure that they re-emerge intact and are edified, not diminished.

Parenting is not about winning or losing; it is about staying connected and growing in relationship to your child, yourself, and the mysteries of the relationship as it unfolds. You will know if you are successful by the degree to which you are able to stay connected to your children as you move through situation after situation, together.

MINDFUL MIRRORING

P arenting presents the opportunity to start fresh each day. In any moment, we can choose to be who our child needs us to be. The best part is that we don't have to work too hard to figure this out. If we listen, our children will tell us! It is the parent's job to respond, with a smile that greets her as she struggles with a tough concept learned at school, compassionate understanding when she has made a mistake, or heartfelt sorrow when he has been excluded from a group of friends.

Imagine that you are a mirror, a vital and indispensable reflection that your children need in order to clearly see themselves. I am not talking about checking the hair, adjusting the "look." I am talking about really seeing who they are, knowing them and learning the depth of self-acceptance that allows them to find their place in the world. In order for our children to reach their full maturation, they must experience a parent who is present and thus able to be this mirror. This mirroring allows our children to see themselves in our reflection.

As we invent ourselves on a moment-to-moment basis, parenthood is uncovered, recovered, and discovered in our own experience as well as in our child's. Parenthood emerges as we fulfill the day-to-day functional roles of parenting. Who we are as parents is revealed through our willingness to hold a provisional identity, which means that we become who our child needs us to be in every new moment. How we evolve is determined by the degree to which we surrender. Consider this an opportunity. If we really settle into this process, we can rest assured that what we are doing with our life, at least in this moment, is exactly what we need to be doing.

I remember comforting my infant in the middle of the night, taking a nap with my two-year-old on a summer's afternoon, and later, when he was a teenager, picking him up from a party when he called to tell me that he "made a mistake and drank too much." Even when I found myself writing a check for his college tuition, I realized something quite profound: *this is what I am meant to be doing.* Those moments and actions, though very different, are each exactly what I am here to do.

Being a present parent requires a good measure of *mindfulness*. When we are mindfully parenting, we do not know beforehand what the next moment will bring. Each moment with our child is a gift. We cannot be preoccupied or rely on a rigid structure of who we are or what we think we know. We have to feel, listen, receive, and be willing to give consciousness to the demands of this moment. We have to be open, pliant, and receptive to what the next moment may bring. As the moments flow, they burst with an immense potential for the unexpected. This demands an embodied generosity and a sacrifice of self in relation to our children. We must put other conflicting needs on hold in order to receive these moments. This is parent-mindfulness.

A present parent is mindful of their self while being aware of holding the child in a sustained flow of consciousness without diminishment of either the parent's or the child's thoughts and feelings. This process is both intra-personal and inter-personal and carries enormous transformative potential between parent and child.

Whether you intend it or not, you are introducing your child to the world in everything you do, say, or even think because your child is aware of you and taking you in with every breath. In these observed moments, you are participating as she slowly patterns a way of being. You are her mirror.

NURTURE

L et's look closer at one of today's parenting paradoxes: these days, parents are both providers outside of the home and nurturers within the home. To provide, we must be strong and able to move outside ourselves to interact with the world. To nurture, we must be vulnerable and willing to tend to the needs of others.

As parents, we have to chart a course between being together and being apart. Though we are responsible for fulfilling the role of nurturer, we may not always feel nurturing. We may want to keep watching the game, get ready for work, finish a phone call, or simply be left alone. In any given moment, our needs may be in opposition to the needs of our child. Seeking a balance is almost always going to create a challenge.

Your child may have to wait for you to respond while you complete a thought, conclude a text, or finish reading an article. He may simply have to wait while the bottle is being prepared or tolerate your struggle to understand what he is saying. On the other hand, you may suspend your activity and immediately respond, but this could leave you feeling frustrated or incomplete. In either case, how the tension is negotiated, balanced, and resolved is the basic ground of parenting.

Through a very intentional presence, parents can evoke a "container of presence" that holds and facilitates the development of their children. This container also holds their relationship in a safe place. The parent is a significant architect in building and holding the infrastructure of "home." It is not necessarily a place where the child wants to be all the time but a place where she brings her experience of the outer world back for sharing and integration.

The concept of "home" is constructed and experienced physically by the child at an early age. As the child develops, home shifts to live within them. Nurturing is an implicit agreement to hold the context of home and the significant responsibilities that go along with it.

When your child raises his head, looks in your direction, beams recognition, or runs to you, what you do in that moment is very important. How you respond communicates something about the place that he occupies within your world. It tells him who he is to you. If he is coloring, does he have to run to you to show you his drawing? Or do you put down whatever burden you are carrying, go to him, sit on the floor, and open to the wonder of his moment? As he sits behind you in the car seat and talks, are you listening? And when he glances toward you on the sidelines, do your eyes let him know that you see him? Does he see in your eyes the warmth of recognition, or, because you are distracted and busy with your own concerns, is something conveyed that he cannot comprehend? As parents, we must always choose how we intend to embrace our child's world. In doing so, we nurture: we show them that they exist, they matter, and they have a place not only inside of us but in the greater world as well. Our children build an entire library of "movies" resulting from memories of the experiences we have together or apart. As parents, we need to make the adjustments necessary to ensure that we stand beside them in as many of those moments as possible and enable them to flourish, which is exactly what it means to nurture.

Be **Open** and Observant

Parenting is not an easy job. Staying present, observant, and open is not an easy choice. You know the moments: your child is describing—for the fifth time—an experience she had at school; your teen wants to know—for the tenth time—if her shirt is the right one to wear tonight; your toddler wants to play Go Fish—for the fifteenth time. You desperately want to get up, turn on the TV, check your phone, or open your laptop. We've all been there.

Making conscious choices to stay open is a daunting task. But who is better equipped to manage these moments: you or your child? As my son matures and is faced with situations that force him to experience what he is feeling—an argument with his girlfriend, a lost buddy, a paper that he has put off to the last moment—he needs to find his way into and through these emotions as I stand in the background, observing and willing to step into operational mode when needed. If I move away from these situations and defend against having to feel my own emotions because I am busy, distracted, judgmental, or unwilling to manage my thoughts and feelings, then I inadvertently teach him to do the same.

Every situation with your child presents the opportunity for you to stay with them. In other words, every moment your child interacts with you is an invitation to participate in their world. You have the choice to either accept or decline. If you decline this invitation, you create separation, but when you accept, you open up another chance to stay connected and experience a deep and lasting bond.

Tips for Staying Open and Observant

- **Be willing to observe and learn about yourself**, and be open to your limitations. This is one of the enormous gifts that having children provides.
- **Understand that the choices you make directly impact your child, always.**

↬ **Try to stay with the moment while managing any impulses that might close you down and pull you away.** Coming and going is the obvious part of parenting. This happens all day long. Learn how to stay with it.

↬ **When you feel like it is time to move on, stay longer.** All things will come to an end, of course, so investigate what it would be like if you were willing to stay with it a little longer. A few extra precious moments with your child can make all the difference in the quality of your connection.

↬ **The key is to meet your child's needs while simultaneously meeting your own.** Keep an open dialogue explaining the importance of both.

↬ **Be proactive.** Don't wait until the demands of the day come looking for you.

↬ **Show up on time and let it be all about them.** Even when they resist, be present. Stick with it, and stick with them. Try to be there in the morning when they wake up and at night when they go to sleep.

↬ **Get to know their friends.** Inquire about them on a regular basis. This might be met with "Why do you want to know?" But the response doesn't matter; what does matter is that you are interested, another indication of your presence. Support the value they find in all of their relationships.

⊸ **Even if they don't return your calls or texts, persist and maintain open communication.** Many times, when it is difficult to reach your child, they are reflecting: processing their own thoughts and emotions so that when they do finally reach out, something important emerges.

Many of us are doing everything we can to connect with and stay open to our children. We do this willingly while also managing very complex feelings. As a parent, it is entirely common to have ambivalence. You want to be here, yet you are compelled to be elsewhere. You want to hold and nurture, and yet you feel the pain of not receiving this in kind. In any given moment, you might feel pulled in a million different directions. Our internal world of thoughts, feelings, and memories can interrupt our ability to listen to and take in our children. Parents of young children endure this ambivalence on a daily basis. Combating it takes patience and an open heart.

Our children will teach us everything we need to know about ourselves if we are willing to trust the situation, trust our children just the way they are, and resolve to include all of who we are as a parent in every moment. If we can find a way to stay open to the full challenge of parenting as life continues to unfold, we can then grow together.

PROVIDE AND BE PATIENT

With the rise of single-parent households and mixed-gender parental functions, parenting is no longer viewed as only the work of "mother and father." Sometimes, this can make it even more difficult to manage the responsibilities of work and home. No matter where you fall on this spectrum, your role as a parent is to provide for and be patient with your child's ever-shifting needs.

Clearly, this is easier said than done. Being patient can take its toll on our psyches, especially when we're out of practice. You're not alone if you've felt frustration or even sparks of anger while trying to remain patient. Take heart. The actual root of the word patience means "to suffer." This practice is not meant to be a cakewalk. It can be seen as an opportunity to develop inner peace in the midst of chaos. Developing patience is a lifelong process; parenting just makes it a daily priority.

We are all navigating the stress of managing dual-income or single-income households while being present for our work and for our children. So how do we remain calm enough to be patient for the capricious needs of our child from one moment to the next? When given permission to struggle with the psychological, emotional, and logistical challenges of parenting, we can find a way through the difficulty, achieving an outcome that becomes mutually beneficial.

Simply put, I have to trust my child, our relationship, and each moment we experience together. This trust is based on an understanding that if I stay in it long enough and feel what I have to feel to maintain the connection, I will find a way through the challenges. Being patient involves a willingness to take a leap of faith, slow down, and manage my emotions while maintaining a continuous engagement with my child.

Q.1

LIVE THE **QUESTIONS**

Being a present parent is *not* about knowing the answer. By now, you're aware that it's about living the questions—those your child asks you in any given moment and the ones you ask yourself. Here are a few, but the list goes on forever.

Am I doing this right?

Am I making too many mistakes?

Will my child suffer because I don't always know the best answer?

How will this action affect my child?

How will I know the outcome of this situation is for my child's highest good?

Will I suffer, or worse, will my child suffer because I'm less than perfect?

Hopefully you are chuckling at the last question. Though we pose it to ourselves from time to time, we know it's impossible to answer because there is no such thing as a perfect parent.

The closest we can get to the illusion of "perfection" is to be present. We know that maintaining presence is real because when we are genuinely present, we feel a deeply seeded bond with our children and ourselves. There is nothing more calming to the agitated mind than this feeling.

The good news is that when we parent, we can notice when we've disappointed or failed our children, and we can investigate what was internally activated to precipitate this failure. If we are willing to show up and feel, we can better support our children.

Perhaps the best way forward is simply to keep the questions alive. When a child asks a question, you have three options: pontificate, ask them what they think, or live into the question with them. I'm certain that some of us have been waiting our entire lives to "teach the world what we know," whether it is about how an airplane rotor turns or why we stir the batter in a certain way. It is only when we let go of trying to have all the answers, for ourselves and for our children, that we are able to move that much more firmly into authentic presence. In the process of learning, it is helpful for children to articulate their own thoughts. This is a delicate balance. At some point, we must stop with our need to appear wise and simply ask: "What do *you* think?"

RESPONSIBILITY

The day you found out you were going to have a baby was either one of the most exciting or most terrifying—probably both. With a child on the way, you realized you were about to be responsible for another person's entire life. The responsibility inherent in parenting can be daunting, for obvious reasons.

A child has chosen you to be their parent, and everything they do becomes a reflection of your parenting. Our children become our mirrors, for better or for worse. When bringing a child into the world, you are signing up, consciously or not, to take a closer look at yourself. For many of us, that can be terrifying.

What if we find we're not up for the task? It's not as though we can return a child. I laugh as I type this because I'm sure there are plenty of parents out there who have had this thought, especially during the early stages of infancy when you're trying to navigate the sleepless nights and chaos of tending to a newborn. But this is the very time when the undertaking is clear: your baby is not a pet. This new being is a human whose every breath is dependent on you. This life-and-death dependency is nature's brilliant mechanism to sober us to the enormous responsibility we assume as parents. Without it, I doubt our species would ever survive.

What does it mean to be responsible? The dictionary will point to reliability and dependability. Whether your child is an infant, a toddler, a preteen, a teenager, or a young adult, you, the parent, need to be responsible. You are the one who has to be reliable. You are the one your child needs to depend upon. The guidelines below will help you navigate this enormous task.

- **Responsibility needs to be coupled with control.** It is only when your child is developmentally ready to make choices about what is happening to them that they can be held *response*-able. Once this capacity is developed, we can begin to hold them accountable.

- **Only give your child as much responsibility as he or she can handle.** We have to measure each moment to see if our child will be able to successfully accomplish what we are asking of them.

Otherwise, we are setting them up for failure. I was never big on the theory that "once you set a limit, you must reinforce it." I believe in clear boundaries, but I also experience life as constantly shifting and changing. Parenting a child is one long negotiation where rules are meant to be broken and mutual understanding must prevail. If your child is not successful at being responsible, he most likely agreed to or was forced to do something that was not yet workable. If he could do it, he would—trust him.

- **Provide the example, and they will figure out the rest.** After playtime is over, who should put the toys away? Do we insist that our children take on this responsibility? Do we share this task with them?

- **Provide a context to learn about responsibility.** Make a game out of feeding the dog. Give your child the credit card the next time you are out to dinner and let her calculate the tip and sign. When you need to add a quart of oil to your car, fill the windshield fluid, or put air in the tire, let her do it as you stand by. Trust your children to learn; they are much better at it than we are. Our job is to provide the best context and resources we can afford.

↳ **Children can tolerate "no" to some degree.** "No" sets limits, establishes boundaries, and can even create safety. But too much "no" gives your child a sense that something is wrong within. He will try to do what is right, but if it is met with too much stress and too much negation, he or she will eventually run out of steam. When the thought *I am wrong . . . there is something wrong with me* prevails, it will eventually erode a child's ability to respond.

Children are easily shamed and will quickly make themselves responsible for any discord with their parents. If you are upset, distant, or uninterested, your child will not wonder what is wrong with you—she will wonder what is wrong with her.

Sustaining Support

The very definition of the word "support" represents a litany of actions: to keep stable, to bear weight, to sustain financially, to give active help, encouragement, assistance, or comfort, or to enable something to live. When I say *support your child*, I mean all these things, especially the last—with your support, you enable your child to live.

Supporting our children is not an easy thing to do. It was not easy for my parents, it is not easy for me, and it is not always going to be easy for you. Failure is inevitable. We will fail as a parent more times than we can count. We are finite and limited, and sustaining connection and meeting the expectations of our children is a challenge that does not necessarily always have a happy ending. This will be especially true if your relationship with your parents was challenging.

Support is defined by the receiver, not by the giver. You may feel that you are the most supportive parent in the world; however, if your daughter does not feel supported by you, this is not her fault. You must understand what behaviors and attitudes support your children. Then you must do them, again and again. You will know in their eyes, in their smiles, in their bodies, and in their behaviors when you are hitting the mark.

You are always in your child's life. She will look for you even when she knows you are not there. She may know that you are not coming to her game, but she will see you through the eyes of her teammates as they see their parents on the sidelines. Each time she looks for you, her feelings, thoughts, joys, and disappointments become woven into all of her relationships. This goes on in your absence as well as your presence. If you intend to actively parent, then the most important thing to do is to simply make sure your child knows where you stand in relation to her in any given moment.

But how can you show up, again and again? The very thought can be overwhelming. The answer, though, is very simple. You can only address this challenge one situation at a time. Each time you have the opportunity to show up, trust in your ability to be present. You know what presence is and how to create it. The key to sustaining this presence is to simply do it again and again.

It is never too late to show up, even if you've been absent for years. Your child will always be your child, even when they become adults. They will need you for the challenges that their unique life will inevitably present—loss of lovers, jobs, status, friends, etc. Don't think that being a good parent is letting them continue to "figure it out on their own." Let your child come to you to seek help, and when they do, offer it up in spades. There is no point in cutting them off and causing your child to feel ashamed because they are struggling. You can parent for the rest of your life, through all the stages that parenting presents.

Parenting an adult child demands keeping boundaries and respecting theirs as you respect yours. Offer advice only when they ask for it instead of freely dispensing it without a filter because you think it's what they need to hear. When you show up and are present, you cannot assume that just because this time is convenient for you and your schedule, it will work for your child. Your child also has a life and wants you around when *she* wants you around. The patience you developed while your children were young will require restraint as they mature and become parents themselves.

On that note, it's impossible to meet all of your child's expectations—especially when you're not even sure what they are. When your absence is explained, she may be disappointed, but at least she can fully understand. She can then anticipate how she is going to feel and make the necessary adjustments. Your child does not have a way to keep you out of her heart; everything you do or don't do can affect her.

Say what you do and do what you say. Keep your agreements and make your actions predictable and fair.

Taking on the moment and unraveling its knots is a constant opportunity when you parent. Every day presents a parent the opportunity to show up. No one can tell you how to prepare for the next parenting moment. Take the time to be alone with your children and play with the possibilities that feel right to you.

To build for the future, we must build our foundation strong, from the ground up, and *stay with it*. At a very early age, perhaps too early, a child will begin to realize that his or her growth and development requires moving beyond the world of you, the parent. This realization grows even more over time. While some helpful knowledge and wisdom is passed from one generation to the next, a cultural and societal evolution occurs simultaneously. This can make it difficult for the parent to supply their child with everything that they will need to navigate an ever-changing world.

Prepare yourself each day for the journey. If your participation today was not to your satisfaction, start over tomorrow. We may not be able to control what happens to our children in the future, but we can support them as they greet their future in every moment.

SMOOTH TRANSITIONS

C hildren experience most of their challenges during transitions. Problems arise getting from "here to there" or from "there to here"; however, when children are engaged in their activity, secure in their relationship, and free to express who they are, they are more likely to be happy and content. When change is required, the goal is to help them transition with ease.

Living in transition and constantly moving from one thing to the next is not always a "natural" process for a child. They need downtime as much as uptime. There is a difference between life as a *process*—flowing from one moment to the next—and life that accelerates from one *event* to the next. Children will move more readily throughout their day if we ensure that the events remain connected instead of being disconnected from the moment that came before. The experience of moving from one event to the next, though it may seem exciting and stimulating, is vastly different than moving through a continuous flow of engagement.

How does one move through a continuous flow of engagement in an event-centric culture? Realize that as you step into and out of your child's world, you significantly alter the reality in which they find themselves. Sometimes this is a great thing for a child. When you pick them up after school, they may run excitedly into your arms, but other times, you may not be as immediately welcomed. It's up to you to read the signs and insert yourself appropriately. Just as your child needs time to transition, so do you.

Tuning in to these transitions requires a level of sensitivity and patience that doesn't often come easily, especially for parents who are away from their children for much of the day. Many parents go to work every morning whether they want to or not, and coming home can be one of the biggest transitions. If you have limited time together, it is even more important that you become aware of how you enter and disengage. Often, you might be coming off of long hours, flexing very different muscles than the ones you will use at home. When you return each evening, are you ever really prepared for instant involvement with your children, partner, and family? How do you successfully transition from one side of life to the other? Do you remember that you also need time to make a transition?

Picture yourself outside your front door. Walking through the door does not necessarily mean that you are ready for what awaits. To be successful, this transition requires a good measure of mindfulness.

What do you do in this moment to make a mindful transition? Check in with yourself. What is your energy like? What are you carrying, literally and metaphorically? What do you want to bring with you as you open that door, and what do you want to leave behind? If you are feeling tired and wishing you could have some alone time, are you able to reconnect with your love for your family and accept that your alone time will come a bit later? What is the difference between arriving ready to be home with your family and arriving hoping to continue working? How do you greet your child's joy, even if you are feeling wound up and in work mode?

Take a breath before opening the door. This breath is what separates the past from the future, and it gives you access to the moment.

If your motive is to get your child to do something, you will behave much differently than if you're simply trying to connect. Try to consciously connect before initiating change. Once you have connected, you are better able to engage, explain transitions, and create gentle edges instead of disrupting the moment without warning or explanation.

Facilitating this connection doesn't require complexity. It can be as simple as sitting with your child for ten minutes without the distraction of a screen. How many of us ever take time to pause? Our children need us to teach them the vital importance of pausing and, in so doing, learn to deftly manage transitions.

One simple practice to help children successfully make a transition is to keep it predictable. Explain the moment-by-moment play, and show your child what is going to unfold before it actually happens. This orients a child and allows them to ground themselves. Remind your child of the transition before it happens, and then on the way to school or childcare drop-off, remind them again of your plan. *When I see you later today, we're going to sit on the bench and have a snack.*

Always allow for extra time. Transitions can go awry if not given the proper timing, and we can find ourselves blowing our lids when our patience runs out. Facilitate transitions to mitigate the stress, not add to it.

Give your child plenty of time to complete what they are doing, and be creative about moving on to the next activity. Have a child who opposes the bath? Find a fun way to transport her into the bathroom. Sing. Tell a joke. Does your child fight getting out of pajamas each morning?

Make the transition itself an event—one moment of life moving into the next.

Do whatever you have to do to make these transitions workable so that when you move on to the next "moment" or walk out the door, you do so with a sense of completion and a clear expectation for what is going to happen next.

When I was in clinical training, one of my professors suggested that we focus on every time we walk through a threshold. It could be a passing through a doorway, going down a flight of stairs, or slipping back into our car after dropping our children at school. For each threshold, we were to acknowledge and say good-bye to what was ending and then turn forward and greet what was to come. This powerful practice is worth experimenting with in your own life.

In every transition, there are a series of thresholds; as one thing ends, another begins. We teach our children about life, about change, and about being in the world each time we walk with them through the threshold that says good-bye to what was and hello to what is to come.

TEAMWORK

A
B
C
D
E
F
G
H
I
J
K
L
M
N
O
P
Q
R
S
| T
U
V
W
X
Y
Z

Family life is not an "us or them" situation. It is about how we use our communication with each other to move through the events of our day while staying connected as a family. Working as a family is all about teamwork. Teamwork, when successful, happens because we realize that we are all in this together. Teaching your children to be a part of the team instills the understanding that what affects me affects you and vice versa.

Teaming up with your children requires your willingness to be a part of something larger than you that you can't control. In its truest sense, teamwork places everyone on an equal playing field. In theory, you and your children have equal value and equal say, and everyone is responsible for maintaining the spirit of teamwork. Always remember that you are the parent, and because you are responsible, you have to make sure that what is happening is controllable. So how does this paradox hold true? How are you supposed to be on equal terms yet maintain a sense of authority?

Tips for Teamwork

- ⤷ **Don't be an imposter.** If you ask your children to be a team, show them you are an equal member by participating fully and staying present. Find a way to be authentic and to not act as if you are real if you are not. Don't pretend that something is okay if it really isn't. Don't pretend that something is important if it is not.
- ⤷ **Don't expect more of them than you do of yourself.** Don't ask your child to do something that you are not willing to do.
- ⤷ **Find a way to manage your feelings.** Don't allow how you feel to disrupt your time together. As adults, we need to correctly assess the ever-changing demands of staying together as a team and scale ourselves accordingly. Be the right size for the situation.
- ⤷ **When you are conflicted about having to be present, be present anyway.** It is important to

keep your personal and work life in harmony with your family life.

ↈ **Trust your communication.** You and your children can communicate to find a way to work together. Ask yourself: if you really are on a team with your kids, what is good for the team in this moment? Each moment has a different demand.

If we are teaching our children teamwork so that they will benefit in their out-of-the-family lives, then think about this: When you are part of a team of adults, how do you want to be treated? With clarity, openness, and a sense of mutual respect? If that's what you want your children to receive, then that's what you must be willing to give. If you work as a team, presence becomes something that you can achieve and celebrate together.

U.1.

LET THE MOMENT UNFOLD

As parents, there are countless times when we simply need to stop, breathe, observe, and not interfere with what is unfolding before us. Consider these precious moments.

She is concentrating so deeply on coloring that her tiny pink tongue is protruding from the corner of her mouth. You simply pause, watch her, and allow yourself to be fulfilled.

He is dancing wildly around his room. It is late, you are tired—and you know he is too—yet you stop and hold him compassionately with your awareness. He has to get to bed and you both need to wake up early tomorrow, but for now, all that matters is his frantic display.

She has said something offensive. You are about to respond with justifiable frustration, even anger, but you choose instead to pause, increase your field of understanding, and process the difficult sensation of adrenaline and other hormones running through your veins.

By creating space for you and your child to coexist, each of you is revealed, in the moment, without the driving tension that forces a relational explosion. This "ground" is the terrain of relational life that has a calm center and is the location from which self will emerge.

Parenting with heart, present parenting, suggests a position where the parent stops and provides the calmness and grounding on which the child is held. In this way, the child discovers the part of herself that is unfolding within, moment to moment. The present parent remembers to return to an awareness of balance, equilibrium, and inner peace. This determination becomes a reminder to the parent that there is an innate peace with his child and within their relationship. There is magic in the unfolding, if you allow it.

A
B
C
D
E
F
G
H
I
J
K
L
M
N
O
P
Q
R
S
T
| U
V
W
X
Y
Z

Celebrate the Victory

Celebrate the victory of being present. Successful parenting is not to be measured by the achievements of our children but in the countless moments we sink deeply into the fertile ground of being present with them.

As we surrender, we allow our children to flourish, to fully create themselves in our attention instead of molding them into who they think we need them to be. Only insofar as we are able to open to our experience of our children—our thoughts, our emotions, the experience of being with them—can our children find their own experience of who they are as human beings.

In any moment, know that listening to her, holding him, watching his graceful dance, acknowledging her victory, reading his paper, liking his friend, cleaning up a mess, or simply showing up is absolutely the only thing we need to do to connect our children to their experience.

One moment becomes linked to the next and is held in a framework of mutual understanding. In these moments, our children become a part of our experience and can find our recognition of their participation. We become both the container and the contained. We hold the moment so that the beauty of who we are as parents becomes part of the formation of our children. Achieving this level of presence is a victory worth celebrating.

A
B
C
D
E
F
G
H
I
J
K
L
M
N
O
P
Q
R
S
T
U
| V
W
X
Y
Z

WITNESS THEIR WONDER

O ur children's capacity for wonder, their ability to view almost anything with open-mouthed awe and curiosity—from an ice cream cone to the thousandth airplane flying overhead—is something to honor and hold sacred. Our children teach us how to re-appreciate the miracle of life.

My friend Peter, a talented painter, tells a story that has stuck with him since he was a child. He remembers being at the beach with two friends. One friend in the water calls out to his other friend on the shore, "Come on in. Come in the water!"

The boy on the beach is holding a bright orange in his hand and calls back, "I can't. I am holding this orange!"

Whenever Peter recalls this story, he laughs with deep abandon, even though he has no idea how this made any sense to him fifty years ago. It lives as a question, something unexplained, beyond reason. It lives as a story of children in a world that rejects interpretation.

The story also speaks to the thoughts, beliefs, and conditioning of the adult mind that prevent us from joining our child's world.

So how do we learn to keep their sense of wonder alive and not make them into adults too soon? We can join them in these moments as a sacred opportunity to recognize what we have lost. In any moment, children will both remind us and show us how to be fully alive.

When my son was three, while he played on the computer, my role was to sit and watch. I was plenty busy, between watching him and watching my own intrusive desires to pick up a piece of mail, make a phone call, or do something "more important." He noticed and objected when my attention shifted. I surrendered and watched his fascination. As soon as he became aware of my attention, when I was too focused on him, he pushed me away. As his parent, there seemed to be a prescribed "distance" I was allowed to maintain.

Being held as the center of my world, my son was able to regulate my presence: too little, and he pulled me back to him; too much, and he pushed me away. In this meaningful struggle, I held him as I witnessed him. I participated authentically as part of his world while fending off the impulses to remain in my own. In this interconnected and interdependent context, I sensed a shared feeling of inclusiveness and belonging. In order for his impulses to live, mine became the compost used to nourish the soil of his development, the growth of our relationship, and the web of life that propelled us into the future.

When I think of my son, a young man now, and his journey into the world, I realize that every step of the way, I attempted to walk next to him or, just as often, behind. When he stopped to rest, was confronted with an insurmountable obstacle, or simply needed attention, he could turn around and I would be there. I think about walking next to and behind my child much more often than I think about leading. When he was an infant reaching for something, I would allow him his effort and play. If it became too much of a struggle, I would ease the item within reach. When he was searching for something more, I would walk along and see where his query would lead us. His understanding unfolded through the countless opportunities we shared in his developing world.

W.2

KEEP YOUR **WORD**

Aparent's word becomes the strength and certainty by which a child charts his steps into life.

GUIDELINES FOR KEEPING YOUR WORD

- ✦ **Be accountable.** By staying connected on a day-to-day basis, you become part of the currency of exchange in your children's lives. They live in relationship to you, and you live in relationship to them. Your value is their value, and with this, they negotiate the challenges they face. Do what you say you will do—every time.

- ✦ **Be on time.** Do not keep your child waiting. Write it down in your calendar or your journal. There is no excuse for forgetting.

↪ **Be predictable.** Set clear expectations for both your behavior and your child's. Then actually do it.

↪ **Be consistent.** Communicate your routine so that your children know where to place you in the day. If you are normally home for dinner but will not be tonight, get on the phone or text and let them know. Let this news come directly from you and not through your partner.

↪ **Be familiar.** Create little rituals that are special between you and your child: a special voice for waking them in the morning; a particular way you call out their name when you want their attention. Tell them about your day. Give them a glimpse of the overview of your week. Tell stories about work. Talk about what you are reading.

↪ **Be attentive to the details of their life.** Remember what is occurring in your child's day or week and follow up with them about their friends, tests, classes, teachers, events, etc. Keep up with their life. In the same way that you would remember details about your partner, a dear friend, or an important client, do the same for your child. It is never too late; even if you forgot something that is meaningful to them, you can remember it now. Start over every evening and every morning.

- **Be available when they need you.** Put down the phone, close the computer, turn off the TV, and look at them when they want your attention. Make the effort to listen, even if you think you have heard it all before.

A
B
C
D
E
F
G
H
I
J
K
L
M
N
O
P
Q
R
S
T
U
V
W
X
Y
Z

X.1

GENTLY COAX

When you want your child to do something and he or she is having trouble complying, understand one fact: there is a collision of worlds at play. In moments like these, your child is having difficulty because she is literally in a different context. Her thoughts, behaviors, and meaning structures are not syncing with your world of expectations. If you want your child's attention or compliance, then you must find a way to connect before you direct.

HOW DO YOU DO THIS?

⤷ **Get up out of your chair and go sit with her on the floor** before you inform her that in fifteen minutes, you are both going upstairs to read a story before bed.

- Sit on the side of his bed, gently place a hand on his back, and tell him that in a little while you will be back with some milk and it will be time to wake up.

- Have her help you make the salad so that she is engaged with the food before you expect her to sit at the table and actually eat it.

- Meet your child where they can be found. If your children are in another part of the house and calling them is not working, take a moment to go to them and find out what they are doing. It really is easier than shouting and takes less energy than entering into the consequential frustration.

Make sure to use your behavior, not your voice. While this may seem as though it could take forever, a conscious intention to manage your child ensures that you will get to what needs to happen next, which is a lot more efficient than a collision of worlds. When children melt down or we find ourselves in a tense, argumentative moment, it simply takes up too much time and energy.

If we match our children's energy in these situations—expressing our frustration, anger, or even rage—we only exacerbate the situation. When a child is having difficulty, it's because a current need is not being met. As parents, there is always a choice in how to best respond. In highly charged moments, it is nearly impossible for a child to take in any form of logic, and most efforts will only fall on deaf ears. When their emotional cortex is flooded, they have difficulty rationalizing.

I understand that you want dessert now. I know how much you love dessert. By simply mirroring their desire and remaining a steadfast witness, your children become aware that they have been seen, their request has been heard, and their needs are being respected. Your presence, in and of itself, allows them to hear what it is you have to say next.

Proceed with the intention of always starting with a "yes" and experiment with your method of managing your child's "no." Motivating our children is not an easy task. Once you learn one strategy, another is required. I pass this rule onto you: don't get angry, and don't take "no" for an answer. Something will have to give if you are willing to show up, do the job, and take what you get. Finding a way that works takes a lot of effort, and your attempts are a sign that you care. Conscious and creative solutions are the fibers of your relationship and a measure of your love. Go big for your child. By sharing your presence, you build their future.

SAY "YES"

Find a way to say "yes" to whatever is unfolding. Use patience and understanding to steer your child in the direction you want him or her to go. This requires you to place your children's needs at the center of your consideration. In a very real and tangible way, you have to trust their actions so that you can gently guide them into a world that is beyond their comprehension and control.

This is not easy. The pressures of your day and the demands on your time and patience can often wear thin. It is tempting to listen to the countless voices that speak to you about setting limits, maintaining control, and issuing time-outs. Most people's definition of discipline has something to do with punishing a child when they don't do what we want. In this context, discipline means to assert some idea of order, often interpreted as "do as I say, or else." This method of teaching a child is based on causing them some sort of discomfort or emotional distress when they don't meet our expectations. In the context of present parenting, this is not a wise way to discipline.

Often, we find ourselves disciplining not only because we want to teach our child something or prevent them from harm but because we want to avoid being embarrassed by what other people may think of *us* when our child misbehaves. How many times have you caught yourself wishing your child were behaving differently—saying "thank you" on demand, looking the host of a party in the eye, etc. If we can trace the root of our need to control our child, perhaps this can help us create the space to let go and say "yes"—without causing our child undue pain.

How do you say "yes" while also providing the most conscious level of discipline? As a parent, you are responsible for setting limits with your child. You have to do this to keep them safe and teach them how to participate in a household—and the world.

So how do you manage your child and yourself while helping them understand how to be respectful, cooperative, and safe? It's a lot easier to lead a horse than to try and push it to the proverbial well.

Tips for Saying "Yes"

- ✧ **Disconnect from your expectations** about how you thought this moment should unfold. Create space in yourself and let go. In literal terms, take a deep breath—or three.

- ✧ **Reset your priorities for the short term.** You may leave the house later than you thought. Is it really that big of a deal? Let go of the things you cannot control.

- ✧ **Join your child in whatever they are doing.** If they are not getting out of bed, join them for a moment. If they won't get into the bath, hop in first and get them to follow. If they don't come when you call, stop calling, find them, and make it playful. Then move into the next moment and simply wait for them to join you.

- ✧ **Communicate your expectations and make it about you.** *I need you to come to dinner; I am hungry. I am going to need you to think about me for a minute and understand that I have to go to work after I drop you off at school. Can you tell me what you need right now so that we can take care of you? I need to understand what is going on here.*

Making it about you and what you need communicates a context for them to measure against. It may even build a framework for empathy by subtly teaching them how to articulate their needs as they mature.

- ↝ **Create some space psychically and emotionally.** Step back and give yourself and your child room to breathe. Remember what it was like to be the exact age of your child and imagine a similar moment.

It is not all that difficult to say "yes." It only requires the willingness to do so. *Yes* is a pair of gentle hands versus a grab, a push, a hit. *Yes* is a moment of patience when your child struggles to understand. *Yes* is an acceptance of her frustration when things are not moving according to her plans. *Yes* is not pointing out the obvious when it is too revealing to bear. *Yes* is holding him when he cries at any time of night. *Yes* is leaving something unsaid even when you desperately want to remind him to drive safely or try harder. *Yes* is simply yes to all that she is and can be.

THE CHILD ZONE

A child's sense of smell has a potential far greater than ours. Their sense of taste is so developed that it is common, if you listen, to hear your child reference the taste of color. Their eyes take in everything around them: ants as they parade across the floor, birds as they soar, a white speck in an infinite blue sky. Children live in a world where sounds are not separate from the image or the thoughts connecting them. The child zone is a beehive of activity. If we listen closely, we may hear the hum while they live within the dynamic activity of it all.

Children live in a timeless world of possibility. The very phenomenon that children don't know what time is helps us to be present with them. They remind us again and again that the only time that actually exists, and matters most, is the moment at hand.

In order to help our children learn how to manage time, we have to understand the topography of our child's world: the child zone. Adults think primarily in terms of deadlines and results, while children think about infinite possibility and the freedom to play, dream, and create.

Scheduling our children based on *our* expectations never works. Forcing them to relate to time through our lens will most likely lead to a struggle. Playing the "parent as cop" may achieve results, but it rarely rewards anyone involved.

Moments unfold differently in a child's world: hours can feel like minutes and seconds like hours. "Hurry, Daddy; we have been driving forever." Children often find their parents' expectations around timing very limiting. When they hear, "Hurry up; you will be late for school," the frustration behind our words lands like the boots of a paratrooper in a garden of sweet peas. What is two minutes, really? Imagine if you allowed an extra two minutes to get out the door. Better yet, maybe you rise a little earlier in the morning. Perhaps you get your children out of bed with plenty of time to spare.

At any age, a child, left to their own way, is not connected to the time and space continuum necessary for them to make a smooth transition. It isn't that they are deficient in some way; their minds are simply considering possibilities that adults don't even imagine.

If we patiently and consistently support our children in making successful transitions, then a schedule becomes co-created. How we manage time in our life will determine how seamlessly we teach our children to manage time in theirs. Maintaining a "child zone" mindset helps both of you to navigate the day-to-day trajectory of your lives and prepares everyone to handle even the most unexpected moments with ease.

CONCLUSION

Children are not equipped to make the journey from childhood to adulthood on their own. They need to test themselves, over and over, moment to moment, in a safe environment as they experience themselves for who they are. The successful journey into adulthood, which is very long and arduous for many children, requires that they not carry this weight alone. They need someone or some place to hold their burdens; otherwise, when their age declares they have arrived developmentally, their hearts, emotions, and wounds compel them to remain behind. Parents bring the light of the world into the home by illuminating an outside social structure that is safe and protected.

Children who grow up with present parents approach life in a generous, trusting, and caring manner. Their daily success is enhanced because they simply have to struggle less. Even more so, when they do encounter a struggle, they will be better able to trust themselves, their parents, and the world. Present parenting is not about taking away the inevitable messiness of life. It's about fortifying our children with the ability to manage those vagaries, challenges, and tragedies that are part of the human condition. Our children will have the unencumbered freedom to face the challenges of their developing lives.

We know that children evolve a greater sense of empathy in relation to a present parent. As a result of that relationship, they will develop a genuine and unimpeded capacity to experience and care for the thoughts and the feelings of others. Perhaps this capacity in our children to love and be loved is the ultimate measure of our presence—and success.

When I think about present parenting, I recall a well-known parable:

> *Once upon a time, a master potter was trying to develop a new glaze for his porcelain vases. In fact, it had become the central focus of his entire life. Every day, he meticulously tended to the flames of his kiln, adjusting the temperatures to an exact degree.*
>
> *Every day, he tinkered with the recipe, adjusting the ingredients in an attempt to find the perfect glaze. Still, after many, many attempts, he was*

unable to achieve the beauty he both desired and knew was possible.

Having tried everything, he finally decided that his important and meaningful life was over. Abruptly he walked into the molten heat of his carefully tended kiln.

Later, when his students opened the kiln and removed the vases, they found on every vase the most exquisite glaze they had ever encountered. It was then that they discovered their master, himself, had disappeared into his creations.

As parents, we have this capacity to offer ourselves fully to our children in every moment. Controlling our temperature to just the right degree, we balance each relational moment in a safe and facilitated context so that the beauty of who we are becomes the very basis for the complex formation of our children.

When we enter the molten heat, over and over again, we offer ourselves to each moment's creation. And when we re-emerge, we find that we are incrementally integrated into our children's creative selves, in the most exquisite of all glazes.

As present parents, we find ourselves more often than not disappearing into the very dynamic we are responsible for creating. Even when we cease to be, we will live on as our children's parent.

About the Author

DR. TIMOTHY DUKES is a veteran psychotherapist, leadership advisor, and father. He consults in a variety of institutional settings, working with established business owners, political visionaries, and emerging innovators. His unique program for individual and organizational development—distilled from forty years of clinical work, academic research, and contemplative practice—resolves contradiction and opposition through a clarity-based evolutionary practice. Dr. Dukes maintains a website detailing his work at www.drtimothydukes.com.

About Familius

Visit Our Website: www.familius.com

Join Our Family
There are lots of ways to connect with us! Subscribe to our newsletters at www.familius.com to receive uplifting daily inspiration, essays from our Pater Familius, a free ebook every month, and the first word on special discounts and Familius news.

Get Bulk Discounts
If you feel a few friends and family might benefit from what you've read, let us know and we'll be happy to provide you with quantity discounts. Simply email us at orders@familius.com.

Connect
Facebook: www.facebook.com/paterfamilius
Twitter: @familiustalk, @paterfamilius1
Pinterest: www.pinterest.com/familius
Instagram: @familiustalk

FAMILIUS

The most important work you ever do will be within the walls of your own home.

CPSIA information can be obtained
at www.ICGtesting.com
Printed in the USA
FSOW03n0342230717
36623FS

9 781945 547133